Dedication

This book is dedicated to all those intrepid souls embarked on the profound journey of self-improvement. To the seekers, the dreamers, and the relentless pursuers of personal growth—may the wisdom within these pages illuminate your path, inspire your endeavors, and guide you through the intricate dance of self-discovery.

In honouring the spirit of exploration and the pursuit of higher understanding, this dedication is a tribute to your resilience, courage, and unwavering commitment to becoming the architects of your own destinies. May The Kybalion Code be a beacon on your transformative journey, offering insights, inspiration, and the timeless principles that resonate with the eternal quest for self-mastery.

To each individual navigating the labyrinth of personal growth, this book is dedicated with utmost reverence and gratitude. May your journey be enriched, your spirit uplifted, and your evolution toward self-realisation be both profound and fulfilling.

"Inscribed within the cosmic fabric, The Kybalion Code beckons the discerning seeker to unravel the profound symphony of existence. Within these sacred verses, ancient wisdom weaves an intricate tapestry of principles, each resonating with the eternal rhythms of the universe. As you embark upon this transformative journey, consider these principles not merely as words on paper but as resonant notes that harmonise the dance of life.

In the grand symphony of existence, The Kybalion Code serves as a guide, a celestial score that intricately blends Mentalism, Correspondence, Vibration, Polarity, Rhythm, Cause and Effect, Gender, and the Alchemical Process. These principles are not static commandments but dynamic keys, unlocking the gates to a deeper understanding of self and cosmos.

As you delve into the echoes of ancient melodies, may these principles become the compass directing your path toward self-discovery and mastery. Picture each principle as a luminous star in the vast cosmic expanse, offering guidance through the complexities of your journey.

Let The Kybalion Code be your companion in the quest for wisdom, a repository of timeless truths that transcend the constraints of time and space. As you navigate its verses, envision yourself as an alchemist, transforming the base elements of your existence into the gold of self-realisation.

As you open these pages, allow the resonance of these principles to awaken the alchemist within. Let them stir the depths of your consciousness and illuminate the shadows of the mind. May you find in these words not just wisdom but a symphony of enlightenment, an invitation to dance with the cosmic energies and orchestrate a life aligned with universal harmony. The Kybalion Code is not a mere text; it is an ancient melody, a cosmic dance, and a guide to the profound mysteries that lie within and beyond."

WAYNE DEVLIN BCAA

THE KYBALION CODE

Unlocking Personal Mastery through Ancient Hermetic Principles

Wayne Devlin

Kindle Direct Publishing

kindle direct
publishing

CONTENTS

PREFACE

Navigating the Cosmic Currents

Welcome, fellow seeker, to the sacred realm of The Kybalion Code, a journey into the heart of ancient wisdom that pulsates through the very fabric of existence. As you stand on the threshold of this metaphysical adventure, consider this preface as a compass, guiding you through the cosmic currents that weave the tapestry of this profound exploration.

The Kybalion Code is not just a book; it is a timeless portal that beckons you to explore the fundamental principles governing the universe. These principles, extracted from the Hermetic teachings, are the threads connecting the macrocosm to the microcosm, the celestial to the terrestrial, and the mystical to the mundane.

In this sacred text, we delve into the esoteric realms of Mentalism, Correspondence, Vibration, Polarity, Rhythm, Cause and Effect, Gender, and the Alchemical Process. These are not mere abstractions but living keys, each unlocking a door to a deeper understanding of the self and the cosmos. As you embark on this journey, open your mind to the possibility that the universe is a grand symphony, and The Kybalion Code is your score—a guide to harmonising with the cosmic melodies that reverberate through time and space.

This preface serves as an invitation to approach the text with an open heart and a curious mind. The Hermetic principles are bridges connecting ancient wisdom to the contemporary seeker. Whether you are well-versed in esoteric knowledge or taking your first steps into the mysteries of the universe, let this be a collaborative journey—an exploration that transcends time, culture, and individual perspectives.

Consider The Kybalion Code as a living scripture, a repository of perennial truths that have guided seekers through the ages. As you immerse yourself in these pages, let the wisdom contained herein spark the alchemical fire within, illuminating the path to self-discovery and mastery.

May your journey through The Kybalion Code be transformative, enlightening, and filled with the awe of cosmic revelation. The universe awaits your exploration, and within these principles, you hold the keys to unlocking the secrets of existence.

With an open heart and an inquisitive spirit, let us embark together on this odyssey through The Kybalion Code, a sacred text that transcends time to offer timeless guidance in the ever-unfolding dance of life.

◆ ◆ ◆

Numerous self-help books dedicated to personal development have been penned throughout the years, yielding a spectrum of outcomes. In the realm of lifestyle philosophies, myriad ideas emerge, capturing attention momentarily only to fade into obscurity soon after. These transient ideologies seldom withstand the test of time. Yet, amidst the flux, there exists a perennial wellspring of wisdom that traces its roots back to ancient civilizations, including the venerable era of the Egyptians.

The unbroken thread of knowledge emanates from certain Hermetic systems of thought, resiliently translated and adapted across epochs, particularly thriving in the tapestry of New Age philosophies. An exemplary embodiment of this enduring wisdom is found in "The Kybalion," a work that distils complex philosophical underpinnings into an accessible form. This text not only simplifies ancient teachings but also serves as a guide for contemporary seekers, offering a timeless system of self-help insights.

The Kybalion Code, an elucidating companion to The Kybalion, meticulously dissects this philosophical framework. By delving into its pages, one can unravel a comprehensive system designed to navigate the intricacies of modern life. The text not only decodes the wisdom embedded in ancient Hermetic principles but also elucidates practical steps for achieving a harmonious and balanced existence. In essence, it unveils a blueprint for self-help that transcends temporal boundaries, providing a roadmap for those seeking equilibrium and fulfilment in the complexities of the contemporary world.

Therefore, The Kybalion Code stands as a testament to the enduring relevance of ancient wisdom, showcasing how a profound understanding of timeless principles can be applied to the challenges and opportunities of the present. As readers engage with this text and decipher its messages, they embark on a transformative journey that transcends eras, offering profound insights and actionable steps toward achieving a balanced and purposeful life.

◆ ◆ ◆

THE KYBALION CODE

Unlocking Personal Mastery through Ancient Hermetic Principles

Introduction

I n the vast realm of personal development, seekers have delved into ancient wisdom, seeking timeless principles to navigate the complexities of life. "The Kybalion Code" invites you on a transformative journey, drawing inspiration from the profound teachings of "The Kybalion," a hermetic text that unveils the secrets of the universe and the keys to personal mastery.

As we embark on this exploration, it is essential to understand that The Kybalion encapsulates the distilled wisdom of ancient Hermeticism, a philosophical tradition rooted in the teachings of Hermes Trismegistus, the mythical sage and messenger of the gods. Comprising seven foundational principles, The Kybalion provides a comprehensive guide to understanding the fundamental laws governing the universe. These principles are not mere esoteric musings but powerful tools that, when applied, can unlock the door to profound personal transformation.

The Kybalion Code is not a rigid doctrine but a dynamic framework that empowers individuals to harness their inner potential and align with the natural order of the cosmos. In the pages that follow, we will explore each principle, decipher its profound implications, and illuminate practical ways to integrate these timeless truths into our daily lives.

Our journey begins with the Principle of Mentalism, unveiling the power of the mind as the creative force behind all existence. From there, we'll traverse through the Principles of Correspondence, Vibration, Polarity, Rhythm, Cause and Effect, and Gender, each revealing unique facets of the cosmic dance and providing valuable insights into the art of self-mastery.

"The Kybalion Code" is an invitation to transcend the limitations of the ordinary and embark on a quest for self-discovery. As we unravel the mysteries of The Kybalion, we equip ourselves with the tools needed to navigate the complexities of the modern world while fostering personal growth, resilience, and a profound sense of purpose.

So, dear reader, fasten your seatbelt and prepare for an odyssey into the realms of the ancient and the eternal. Let the wisdom of The Kybalion illuminate your path as you unlock the secrets of personal development and embark on a journey toward the highest expression of yourself. The adventure begins now.

PROLOGUE

In the grand tapestry of human existence, there exists an innate longing for understanding—a desire to unravel the mysteries of life, to decode the secrets that govern our journey through time and space. It is within this pursuit that we find ourselves drawn to ancient wisdom, seeking timeless principles that transcend the limitations of the mundane and open the door to profound personal transformation.

"The Kybalion Code" emerges as a beacon in this quest for enlightenment. Rooted in the esoteric teachings of The Kybalion, a hermetic text of unparalleled depth and insight, this book serves as a guide for those who seek not only knowledge but also the practical application of universal truths. The principles laid out in The Kybalion are not relics of a bygone era but living keys that unlock the doors to self-discovery, personal mastery, and the realisation of our highest potential.

As we embark on this exploration, it is crucial to acknowledge that The Kybalion is more than a mere book; it is a distillation of ancient Hermetic wisdom, a philosophical tradition that traces its roots to the mythical Hermes Trismegistus. The Hermetic principles contained within these pages are both profound and pragmatic, offering a roadmap for navigating the complexities of existence while facilitating an intimate connection with the cosmic order.

In "The Kybalion Code," we endeavor to bridge the gap between ancient mysticism and modern personal development. Each chapter delves into a specific Hermetic principle, unraveling its intricacies and deciphering its relevance to our contemporary lives. Through anecdotes, practical exercises, and thoughtful reflections, we aim to make these ageless truths accessible and applicable to the challenges and opportunities of the 21st century.

This book is an invitation to journey beyond the surface of conventional wisdom, to dive into the depths of the mind and the cosmos, and to emerge with a profound understanding of self and the universe. The Kybalion Code is not a rigid set of rules but a flexible framework, inviting readers to explore, question, and apply these principles in ways that resonate with their unique life paths.

As we embark on this odyssey together, let us keep in mind that personal development is not a destination but a continuous, evolving process. May "The Kybalion Code" serve as a trusted companion on your journey, providing insights, inspiration, and practical guidance as you unlock the mysteries of your own potential and chart a course toward personal mastery.

Welcome to a transformative exploration of ancient wisdom for the modern seeker. Your adventure begins now!

CHAPTER 1: THE PRINCIPLE OF MENTALISM - THE CREATIVE POWER OF THE MIND

Introduction to the Principle of Mentalism

I n the labyrinth of existence, where thoughts shape reality and consciousness is the architect of experience, we encounter the foundational principle of Mentalism. It is here, at the genesis of The Kybalion Code, that we explore the profound idea that "The All is Mind; the Universe is Mental." This principle posits that the ultimate reality is mental in nature, and everything we perceive and experience is a product of the mind.

Mentalism invites us to transcend the limitations of materialism and recognise the creative power residing within the realm of thought. In understanding that the mind is not confined to the boundaries of the skull but extends beyond, we embark on a journey to unlock the vast potential inherent in our thoughts and consciousness.

Exploring the Concept of the All-Mind

At the heart of the Principle of Mentalism lies the concept of the All-Mind—an omnipresent, infinite intelligence that permeates every atom of the universe. This cosmic mind is the source of all creation, the wellspring from which thoughts flow and manifest into the fabric of reality. Understanding the All-Mind empowers us to recognise our interconnectedness with the cosmos, encouraging a shift in perspective from isolated individuals to co-creators with the universal intelligence.

As we delve into the intricacies of the All-Mind, we discover that our thoughts are not isolated occurrences but threads woven into the cosmic tapestry. The Kybalion beckons us to tap into this universal consciousness, to align our thoughts with the harmonious vibrations of the All-Mind, and to realise the role we play as conscious participants in the ongoing creation of our reality.

Practical Exercises to Harness the Creative Power of the Mind

The journey into the Principle of Mentalism is not a passive exploration but an active engagement with the creative forces that shape our lives. To harness the creative power of the mind, we embark on practical exercises designed to cultivate mindfulness, expand consciousness, and channel our thoughts toward intentional creation.

1. Mindful Meditation

Engage in regular meditation to quiet the chatter of the mind and connect with the stillness within. Through mindfulness, we create a space for conscious thought, allowing us to observe and redirect the flow of our mental energy.

2. Visualisation Techniques

Practice the art of visualisation to vividly imagine desired outcomes. By vividly picturing our goals and aspirations, we align our mental energies with the creative forces of the All-Mind, setting the stage for manifestation.

3. Affirmations and Thought Management

Consciously choose empowering thoughts and affirmations that resonate with your goals. Thought management is a transformative practice, as we mould our mental landscape to reflect the reality we wish to create.

As we engage in these exercises, we not only witness the immediate impact on our mental state but also begin to recognise the ripple effect in the external world. The Principle of Mentalism thus becomes a practical guide to navigating the creative potential within, as we consciously participate in the ongoing process of universal creation.

CHAPTER 2: THE PRINCIPLE OF CORRESPONDENCE - AS ABOVE, SO BELOW

Understanding the Macrocosm and Microcosm

In the vast symphony of the cosmos, the Principle of Correspondence echoes the ancient axiom, "As Above, So Below; As Below, So Above." This profound principle reveals the interconnectedness of the macrocosm (the universe) and the microcosm (individual existence). By understanding the parallelism between these two realms, we gain insights into the universal laws that govern both the celestial and the personal.

The macrocosm, with its galaxies, stars, and cosmic patterns, mirrors the microcosm—the intricate dance of atoms, cells, and energies within our being. Recognising this cosmic resonance, we embark on a journey of self-discovery that transcends the confines of the individual self. As we explore the vastness of the macrocosm, we simultaneously delve into the depths of our own inner cosmos, understanding that the patterns found in the heavens are mirrored within us.

Applying the Principle of Correspondence in Daily Life

The practical application of the Principle of Correspondence is the bridge between the cosmic and the personal. It invites us to consciously align our thoughts, emotions, and actions with the harmonious patterns inherent in the universe. Here, the recognition that our internal state is reflected in our external reality becomes a powerful tool for personal transformation.

1. Reflective Practices

Cultivate self-awareness through reflective practices. Regularly contemplate your thoughts, emotions, and actions, recognising their resonance with universal patterns. In doing so, you open the door to conscious alignment with the cosmic flow.

2. Holistic Decision-Making

Before making decisions, consider their impact on various aspects of your life and the lives of those around you. By understanding the interconnectedness of all things, you make choices that resonate with the higher patterns of the cosmos, fostering balance and harmony.

3. Nature Connection

Immerse yourself in nature, observing its rhythms and cycles. Nature serves as a tangible manifestation of the Principle of Correspondence, offering insights into the harmonious dance of life. By aligning with natural patterns, you enhance your connection with the universal order.

Finding Harmony through
Alignment with Cosmic Patterns

As we apply the Principle of Correspondence in our daily lives, we embark on a journey of seeking harmony—a harmonious relationship with ourselves, others, and the cosmos. This alignment is not a passive surrender but an intentional dance with the cosmic rhythms, a conscious participation in the unfolding patterns of existence.

1. Synchronicity and Flow

Embrace synchronicities and go with the flow of life. Recognise that when you align your thoughts and actions with the cosmic currents, you invite serendipity and meaningful connections into your life.

2. Balance and Equilibrium

Strive for balance in all aspects of your being. Just as celestial bodies maintain their orbits, finding equilibrium in your thoughts, emotions, and actions fosters a sense of inner peace and alignment with universal patterns.

3. Creative Expression

Express your creativity in alignment with the cosmic order. Whether through art, music, or other forms of expression, tapping into your creative flow connects you with the creative forces of the universe.

In embracing the Principle of Correspondence, we discover that the cosmic dance is not distant but intimately woven into the fabric of our being. Through conscious alignment with universal patterns, we find harmony, purpose, and a deeper connection to the eternal rhythms of existence.

CHAPTER 3: THE PRINCIPLE OF VIBRATION - THE COSMIC SYMPHONY

Recognising the Vibrational Nature of the Universe

I n the grand cosmic symphony, the Principle of Vibration unveils the underlying truth that all is in a state of perpetual motion, oscillating at various frequencies. Every atom, every thought, and every emotion resonates with its unique vibration, creating a vast cosmic tapestry of frequencies. By recognising the vibrational nature of the universe, we open the door to understanding the subtle energies that shape our reality.

1. Subatomic Harmony

Dive into the world of quantum physics and explore the dance of subatomic particles. Understand that even seemingly solid matter is, at its essence, a dance of vibrating energy. This realisation transforms our perception of the material world, inviting us to see beyond appearances and acknowledge the dynamic interplay of energies.

2. Energetic Thought Patterns

Reflect on the vibrational quality of your thoughts and emotions. Recognise that your mental and emotional states emit distinct frequencies. By becoming aware of these subtle vibrations, you gain the power to consciously shape your thoughts and emotions, influencing the energetic currents of your life.

Tuning into Higher Frequencies
for Personal Growth

Just as a musician tunes an instrument to achieve harmonious melodies, the Principle of Vibration invites us to tune into higher frequencies for personal growth and transformation. By consciously raising our vibrational frequency, we align ourselves with elevated states of consciousness and expanded awareness.

1. Mindfulness and Elevation

Practice mindfulness to become attuned to your current vibrational frequency. Through awareness, you can gently guide your thoughts toward higher, more uplifting vibrations. Cultivate gratitude, positivity, and love to elevate your consciousness and attract higher vibrational experiences.

2. Intentional Living

Set intentions that resonate with your highest self. By aligning your goals and aspirations with elevated frequencies, you infuse your actions with purpose and draw positive energies into your life. Intentional living becomes a powerful tool for personal growth and vibrational elevation.

Utilising Sound and Resonance for Well-being

Sound, with its profound impact on vibration, becomes a key tool for well-being in the exploration of the Principle of Vibration. From ancient traditions to modern therapies, the use of sound and resonance has been recognised as a potent means to harmonise the body, mind, and spirit.

1. Sound Meditation Practices

Engage in sound meditation practices, such as chanting, singing bowls, or tuning forks. These modalities harness the power of sound to shift your vibrational state, promoting relaxation, clarity, and spiritual connection.

2. Music as Therapy

Explore the therapeutic benefits of music. Choose compositions that resonate with your desired emotional and mental states. Music has the ability to elevate mood, reduce stress, and create an environment conducive to healing and well-being.

3. Resonance in Relationships

Recognise the importance of resonance in relationships. Surround yourself with individuals whose vibrations align with your values and aspirations. Positive relationships create a harmonious resonance that uplifts and supports personal growth.

In embracing the Principle of Vibration, we become orchestral conductors of our own cosmic symphony, attuning ourselves to the frequencies that lead to personal evolution and well-being. By understanding and consciously working with vibrational energies, we unlock the transformative potential of the cosmic dance in our lives.

CHAPTER 4:
THE PRINCIPLE
OF POLARITY -
EMBRACING DUALITY

Navigating the Dance of Opposites

I n the intricate dance of the universe, the Principle of Polarity reveals itself as the cosmic law of opposites. It declares that everything has its polar opposite, and that seemingly contradictory forces are, in fact, complementary aspects of a unified whole. As we navigate the dance of opposites, we come to understand that light and darkness, joy and sorrow, and growth and decay are inseparable partners in the grand cosmic ballet.

1. Awareness of Opposites

Cultivate awareness of the dualities present in your life. Acknowledge that opposing forces coexist and, in many ways, define each other. By recognising the interdependence of opposites, you gain insight into the inherent balance woven into the fabric of existence.

2. Finding Unity in Duality

Explore the idea that polarities are not isolated entities but interconnected elements of a greater whole. Just as a magnet has two poles yet functions as a unified entity, embracing the unity within duality allows you to navigate life's challenges with a sense of equilibrium.

Transcending Dualistic Thinking for Inner Harmony

The Principle of Polarity beckons us to transcend the limitations of dualistic thinking—a mindset that categorises experiences into rigid dichotomies of good or bad, success or failure. By transcending dualism, we open ourselves to inner harmony, recognising that the interplay of opposites is an essential and harmonious aspect of the human experience.

1. Mindful Acceptance

Practice mindful acceptance of both positive and challenging experiences. Rather than labeling events as solely good or bad, acknowledge the spectrum of emotions and lessons that accompany each situation. Through acceptance, you cultivate inner peace in the face of life's fluctuations.

2. Integration of Shadows

Explore the integration of your shadow self—the aspects

of yourself that you may find challenging or undesirable. By embracing and integrating these shadow elements, you move toward wholeness and reduce inner conflict. The light and dark within you coalesce into a unified expression of your true self.

Balancing Polarities in Relationships and Personal Development

Just as polarities exist within ourselves, they also shape the dynamics of our relationships and personal development. The Principle of Polarity invites us to seek balance and integration in these areas, fostering growth, understanding, and harmony.

1. Harmony in Relationships

Recognise the complementary nature of differences in relationships. Embrace diversity of thought and perspective, understanding that opposing views can enrich the tapestry of connections. By finding common ground amidst differences, relationships thrive in a harmonious dance of polarities.

2. Personal Growth through Challenge

View challenges as opportunities for personal growth. Instead of resisting difficulties, acknowledge that they are integral to your journey of self-discovery. Embrace challenges as catalysts for transformation, recognising that the path to growth often involves navigating the interplay of opposing forces.

3. Balance in Decision-Making

Apply the Principle of Polarity in decision-making by considering the interplay of opposing factors. Seek balance in choices, understanding that optimal decisions often involve a thoughtful integration of competing considerations. By balancing polarities, you navigate your path with wisdom and discernment.

In embracing the Principle of Polarity, we learn to dance gracefully with the dualities of life, finding beauty and balance in the ebb and flow of opposites. Through transcending dualistic thinking and harmonising polarities, we unveil the inherent unity within diversity, fostering inner harmony and holistic growth.

CHAPTER 5: THE PRINCIPLE OF RHYTHM - THE EBB AND FLOW OF LIFE

Understanding the Cyclical Nature of Existence

I n the grand orchestration of the cosmos, the Principle of Rhythm emerges as the cosmic dance of cycles, emphasising the inherent ebb and flow that permeates all aspects of existence. From the rising and setting of the sun to the changing seasons, life unfolds in rhythmic patterns. Understanding the cyclical nature of existence becomes a key to navigating the complexities of our personal journeys.

1. Observing Natural Cycles

Cultivate a heightened awareness of the natural cycles surrounding you. Observe the seasons, lunar phases, and the daily rhythms of nature. Recognising these recurring patterns offers profound insights into the cyclical nature of life and the interconnectedness of all things.

2. Life as a Symphony

Envision your life as a symphony of rhythms, each phase contributing to the richness of the whole. Embrace the idea that, like musical notes, experiences rise and fall in a rhythmic cadence. This perspective encourages a sense of acceptance and flow in the face of life's inevitable fluctuations.

Cultivating Resilience through Rhythmic Awareness

The Principle of Rhythm teaches us that challenges and joys are not permanent but transient phases in the grand symphony of life. Cultivating resilience through rhythmic awareness involves adapting to the changing beats, finding strength in times of challenge, and remaining humble during moments of success.

1. Adaptability and Flow

Develop adaptability by recognising that life's challenges are temporary. Like a river flowing through varied terrain, your journey may encounter obstacles, but with adaptability, you navigate them with ease. Embrace the ebb and flow, understanding that change is an integral part of the rhythmic dance of life.

2. Mindful Presence

Practice mindful presence in each moment, acknowledging that both high and low notes contribute to the beauty of the overall composition. By staying present, you build resilience and navigate challenges with a sense of calm and clarity, knowing that the rhythm of life will carry you through.

Synchronising with Cosmic Rhythms for Personal Growth

The awareness of cosmic rhythms invites us to synchronise our personal rhythms with the larger cadence of the universe. By aligning our intentions, actions, and goals with the cosmic pulse, we unlock a powerful pathway for personal growth.

1. Lunar Intentions

Harness the energy of the lunar cycles to set intentions and manifest goals. The moon's phases offer a natural rhythm for introspection, planning, and manifestation. By aligning your intentions with lunar cycles, you tap into the cosmic flow that supports your personal evolution.

2. Seasonal Reflection

Reflect on the changing seasons as metaphors for your own growth. Just as nature experiences periods of dormancy and renewal, recognise the seasons of your life. Use winter as a time for introspection, spring for new beginnings, summer for growth, and autumn for reflection and release.

3. Daily Rhythms of Well-being

Establish daily rhythms that prioritise well-being. Align your activities with your natural energy ebbs and flows, creating a harmonious balance between productivity and rest. By syncing your daily life with your internal rhythms, you enhance overall vitality and personal fulfillment.

In embracing the Principle of Rhythm, we learn to dance with the fluidity of life, riding its waves with grace and resilience. Through understanding the cyclical nature of existence, cultivating rhythmic awareness, and synchronising with cosmic rhythms, we embark on a transformative journey of personal growth within the ever-changing symphony of life.

CHAPTER 6: THE PRINCIPLE OF CAUSE AND EFFECT - THE LAW OF KARMA

Unraveling the Chain of Causation in Life

T he Principle of Cause and Effect, often encapsulated in the ancient concept of Karma, illuminates the intricate web of interdependence woven into the fabric of existence. It asserts that every action, thought, and intention sets into motion a chain of causation, shaping the course of our lives. To understand this principle is to unravel the interconnected threads of cause and effect that govern our individual and collective destinies.

1. Causal Awareness

Develop a heightened awareness of the causes and effects in your life. Reflect on the unfolding events and circumstances, tracing them back to their origins. By acknowledging the interconnected nature of actions and consequences, you gain insight into the underlying dynamics of your experiences.

2. Introspective Inquiry

Engage in introspective inquiry to discern the motives and intentions behind your actions. By exploring the deeper layers of your thoughts and choices, you unearth the seeds of causation that influence your life's trajectory. This introspective process becomes a key to understanding the patterns that shape your reality.

Taking Responsibility for Personal Choices

The Law of Karma emphasises the profound truth that we are architects of our destinies, sculpting our realities through the choices we make. Taking responsibility for personal choices is an empowering acknowledgment that we possess the agency to shape the outcomes of our lives.

1. Ownership of Choices

Embrace the concept of ownership in decision-making. Recognise that, whether consciously or unconsciously, every choice contributes to the unfolding story of your life. By accepting responsibility for your decisions, you reclaim the power to influence and redirect your destiny.

2. Conscious Decision-Making

Cultivate conscious decision-making as a means of shaping

positive outcomes. Consider the potential consequences of your actions before making choices. Through conscious awareness, you align your decisions with your values and aspirations, steering the course of your life in a purposeful direction.

Breaking Destructive Cycles through Conscious Action

The Principle of Cause and Effect offers a pathway to break free from destructive cycles by introducing conscious action into the equation. By understanding that negative consequences arise from harmful actions, we empower ourselves to interrupt detrimental patterns and foster positive change.

1. Mindful Intervention

Intervene mindfully when recognising negative patterns emerging in your life. By interrupting destructive cycles through conscious awareness, you open space for transformation. This may involve acknowledging harmful habits, thought patterns, or behaviors and taking deliberate steps to redirect your course.

2. Karmic Alchemy

Engage in karmic alchemy by transmuting negative energy into positive action. Recognise that every moment presents an opportunity for transformation. By consciously infusing positive intentions and actions into your life, you initiate a process of karmic alchemy that can redirect the course of causation.

3. Generosity and Compassion

Cultivate a spirit of generosity and compassion in your actions. Acts of kindness and compassion not only contribute positively to the world but also create a ripple effect that can break down barriers and transform negative cycles into cycles of goodwill and positivity.

In embracing the Principle of Cause and Effect, we recognise the profound impact our choices have on the unfolding tapestry of our lives. By unraveling the chain of causation, taking responsibility for our choices, and consciously intervening to break destructive cycles, we become architects of positive change and contributors to the greater harmony of the universe.

CHAPTER 7: THE PRINCIPLE OF GENDER - THE DANCE OF MASCULINE AND FEMININE

Embracing the Interplay of Masculine and Feminine Energies

The Principle of Gender unveils the dynamic dance of masculine and feminine energies that underlies the entirety of existence. It acknowledges that these energies are not confined to gender stereotypes but are fundamental forces within each individual. Embracing the interplay of masculine and feminine energies involves recognising and honouring both aspects within ourselves and the world around us.

1. Recognition of Energies

Develop an awareness of the masculine and feminine energies present in your thoughts, emotions, and actions. Acknowledge that both energies contribute to the richness of your being. By recognising their interplay, you unlock a deeper understanding of your inner dynamics and foster a sense of wholeness.

2. Honouring Diversity

Embrace the diversity of masculine and feminine expressions. Recognise that these energies manifest uniquely in each individual, transcending societal expectations. By honouring the diversity of expressions, you contribute to a more inclusive and harmonious understanding of the interplay between masculine and feminine forces.

Balancing and Integrating Gender Energies Within

The Principle of Gender invites us to explore the art of balancing and integrating both masculine and feminine energies within ourselves. Achieving harmony between these energies contributes to a more holistic and authentic expression of our true selves.

1. Inner Alchemy

Engage in inner alchemy by consciously balancing masculine and feminine energies within. This involves recognising areas of imbalance and making intentional shifts toward equilibrium. By cultivating qualities associated with both energies, such as assertiveness and receptivity, you foster a harmonious internal landscape.

2. Wholeness in Expression

Strive for wholeness in your expression of gender energies.

Recognise that embracing both the masculine and feminine within you allows for a more complete and authentic self-expression. This integration contributes to a sense of empowerment and aligns you with the natural flow of cosmic energies.

Fostering Harmonious Relationships through Gender Awareness

Awareness of the Principle of Gender extends to our relationships, where understanding the interplay of masculine and feminine energies can enhance connection, communication, and overall harmony.

1. Communication Styles

Recognise the diverse communication styles associated with masculine and feminine energies. Understanding these differences can foster effective communication in relationships. By appreciating and adapting to each other's communication preferences, you create an environment conducive to understanding and connection.

2. Collaborative Partnerships

Foster collaborative partnerships by embracing the complementary nature of masculine and feminine energies. Recognise the unique strengths each energy brings to the relationship and work together to create a harmonious and synergistic connection. This collaborative approach contributes to shared growth and mutual support.

3. Empathy and Understanding

Cultivate empathy and understanding through gender awareness. Recognise that experiences and perspectives may be influenced by the interplay of masculine and feminine energies. By approaching relationships with openness and curiosity, you create a space for deeper connection and mutual understanding.

In embracing the Principle of Gender, we embark on a journey of self-discovery and relational wisdom. By recognising, balancing, and integrating both masculine and feminine energies within ourselves and fostering gender awareness in our relationships, we contribute to a more harmonious and holistic expression of life's dance.

CHAPTER 8: THE ALCHEMICAL PROCESS - TRANSFORMING THE SELF

*Applying Hermetic Principles
in Personal Alchemy*

The alchemical process, rooted in Hermetic principles, becomes a transformative journey of self-discovery and evolution. By applying these principles in personal alchemy, we engage in the sacred work of refining the raw material of our being into the gold of self-realisation.

1. Understanding the All

Begin by cultivating a deep understanding of the All, the universal consciousness that permeates every aspect of existence. Through the lens of Hermetic principles, recognise that the All is the source of the alchemical process and the guiding force behind personal transformation.

2. Mentalism in Alchemy

Apply the Principle of Mentalism to alchemical work by recognising the power of the mind in shaping personal reality. Your thoughts, intentions, and beliefs become the crucible in which personal alchemy unfolds. By harnessing the creative force of the mind, you guide the alchemical process toward intentional transformation.

Transmuting Challenges into Opportunities for Growth

Alchemy, at its core, is a process of transmutation—turning base elements into gold. In the realm of personal development, this means transmuting life's challenges into opportunities for growth and self-discovery.

1. Alchemy of Adversity

View challenges as the prima materia, the raw material of personal alchemy. Embrace adversity as an essential component of the transformative process. By alchemically working with challenges, you extract the wisdom and lessons they hold, transmuting them into catalysts for growth.

2. Philosopher's Stone of Resilience

Cultivate the philosopher's stone of resilience—the inner alchemical tool that enables you to withstand and overcome challenges. By acknowledging the cyclical nature of life, you foster the strength to endure difficulties and emerge from them with newfound wisdom and resilience.

Cultivating the Philosopher's Stone of Self-Awareness

The philosopher's stone, a mythical substance believed to transmute base metals into gold, serves as a powerful metaphor for self-awareness in the alchemical process. Cultivating self-awareness becomes the cornerstone of personal transformation.

1. Reflective Practices

Engage in reflective practices to deepen self-awareness. Journaling, meditation, and contemplative exercises serve as alchemical tools that allow you to explore the depths of your inner world. Through self-reflection, you uncover the hidden aspects of yourself, bringing them into the light of awareness.

2. Integration of Shadow Self

Embrace the integration of the shadow self—the aspects of your personality that are often overlooked or repressed. The alchemical process involves acknowledging and transmuting these shadow elements. By shining the light of self-awareness on the shadows, you reclaim and integrate them into the wholeness of your being.

3. Transformational Alchemy

Approach self-awareness as a continuous process of transformational alchemy. As you become more attuned to the intricacies of your thoughts, emotions, and behaviors, you unlock the potential for conscious evolution. The philosopher's stone of self-awareness becomes the catalyst for ongoing alchemical refinement.

In the alchemical laboratory of personal development, we embrace the transformative journey of turning the lead of our imperfections into the gold of self-realisation. Through the application of Hermetic principles, the transmutation of life's challenges into opportunities for growth, and the cultivation of the philosopher's stone of self-awareness, we engage in the sacred art of personal alchemy.

CHAPTER 9: THE PATH OF MASTERY - INTEGRATING THE KYBALION CODE

*Synthesising the Principles for
Holistic Personal Development*

As we journey along the Path of Mastery, the time comes to synthesise the principles of The Kybalion into a cohesive framework for holistic personal development. This synthesis involves weaving the threads of Mentalism, Correspondence, Vibration, Polarity, Rhythm, Cause and Effect, Gender, and the Alchemical Process into a tapestry that guides us toward self-mastery.

1. Harmonising Principles

Recognise the interconnectedness of the principles. Mentalism shapes thoughts, Correspondence aligns with purpose, Vibration influences energy, Polarity balances energies, Rhythm guides the pace, Cause and Effect governs choices, Gender integrates energies, and the Alchemical Process transforms challenges. Harmonise these principles into a holistic approach to personal development.

2. Alignment with Cosmic Order

Understand that personal development is not an isolated journey but an alignment with the cosmic order. By synthesising the principles, you create a roadmap that resonates with universal truths. This alignment becomes a guiding light, illuminating the path toward self-realisation and mastery.

Creating a Personalized Roadmap for Self-Mastery

The journey toward self-mastery is highly individual, and creating a personalised roadmap involves tailoring the principles of The Kybalion to your unique path. This roadmap becomes a living document, adapting to your evolving understanding and needs.

1. Identification of Key Areas

Identify key areas in your life that require attention and growth. Whether it is relationships, career, health, or spirituality, pinpoint the domains where you seek mastery. The principles of The Kybalion serve as tools to refine and elevate these areas.

2. Setting Intentions

Set clear intentions for your journey. Define what mastery means to you in each identified area. By establishing specific and measurable goals, you provide a roadmap for your development, aligning your intentions with the universal currents of creation.

3. Application of Principles

Apply the principles of The Kybalion to your roadmap. Mentalism guides your thoughts, Correspondence aligns your actions, Vibration influences your energy, Polarity balances your approach, Rhythm dictates your pace, Cause and Effect shape your choices, Gender integrates your energies, and the Alchemical Process transforms challenges into opportunities.

Navigating Challenges on the Path to Enlightenment

As you tread the Path of Mastery, challenges become inevitable milestones for growth. Navigating these challenges with resilience and wisdom is an integral aspect of the journey toward enlightenment.

1. Mindful Reflection

When challenges arise, engage in mindful reflection. Apply the principles of Mentalism and Cause and Effect to understand the roots of challenges and their impact on your reality. By acknowledging their presence, you lay the foundation for conscious navigation.

2. Adaptability and Resilience

Embrace the Principle of Rhythm by understanding that challenges are part of life's ebb and flow. Cultivate adaptability and resilience as you navigate the rhythmic patterns of adversity.

Recognise that, like the tides, challenges recede, providing opportunities for renewed growth.

3. Alchemy of Transformation

Approach challenges with an alchemical mindset. View them as raw materials for transformation and apply the principles of the Alchemical Process to transmute difficulties into stepping stones toward enlightenment. The philosopher's stone of self-awareness becomes a guiding light in this transformative alchemy.

In the integration of The Kybalion Code, the Path of Mastery becomes a dynamic and personalised journey. By synthesising the principles, creating a roadmap for self-mastery, and navigating challenges with wisdom, you embark on a transformative quest toward enlightenment and holistic personal development.

CHAPTER 10: LIVING THE CODE - A LIFE ALIGNED WITH UNIVERSAL TRUTHS

Real-Life Stories of Individuals Applying The Kybalion Code

I n this final chapter, we delve into the real-life stories of individuals who have wholeheartedly embraced and applied The Kybalion Code to transform their lives. These stories serve as living testimonials to the power and practicality of the principles, illustrating how ordinary individuals have manifested extraordinary results.

1. The Power of Mindful Creation

Explore the journey of Sarah, who, through the application of Mentalism, transformed her career by shifting her thoughts from limitation to possibility. By consciously creating a positive mental landscape, she attracted opportunities that aligned with her aspirations, leading to professional fulfillment and success.

2. Balancing Act of Life Harmony

Follow the story of Alex, who navigated the challenges of work-life balance through the Principle of Polarity. By recognising the interplay of masculine and feminine energies in his daily life, he created a harmonious rhythm that allowed him to excel in his career while nurturing meaningful connections with family and friends.

3. Rhythmic Resilience in the Face of Adversity

Meet Maya, who embodied the Principle of Rhythm during a period of personal adversity. By understanding the cyclical nature of life, she approached challenges with patience and resilience. Maya's story reveals how embracing life's ebb and flow can lead to profound personal growth and transformation.

Practical Tips for Daily Application

Living The Kybalion Code is not a grand gesture but a series of intentional choices made daily. Here are practical tips to incorporate the principles into your everyday life:

1. Morning Reflection

Begin each day with a moment of reflection. Use this time to set positive intentions aligned with your goals, applying the principles of Mentalism and Cause and Effect to guide your thoughts and actions throughout the day.

2. Daily Affirmations

Integrate daily affirmations into your routine. Craft affirmations that resonate with the principles of Vibration and Mentalism, consciously directing your thoughts toward positivity and empowerment.

3. Mindful Pause

Throughout the day, take mindful pauses. Engage in brief moments of reflection, applying the Principle of Rhythm to navigate the ups and downs of daily life with grace and resilience.

4. Express Gratitude

Cultivate a practice of expressing gratitude. By acknowledging the positive aspects of your life, you align with the Principle of Correspondence, attracting more of what you appreciate.

5. Balance and Self-Care

Prioritise balance in your daily activities. Whether through work, rest, or play, embody the Principle of Polarity by finding equilibrium in your daily routine. Practice self-care to ensure holistic well-being.

Inspiring Readers to Embark on Their Own Journeys of Self-Discovery

The stories and practical tips shared in this chapter aim to inspire you to embark on your own journey of self-discovery and transformation. The Kybalion Code is not a set of rigid rules but a guide that adapts to your unique path.

1. Self-Inquiry and Exploration

Begin your journey with self-inquiry. Explore the depths of your thoughts, emotions, and actions, applying the principles of Mentalism and self-awareness. This introspective exploration serves as the foundation for personal growth.

2. Set Intentions for Growth

Set clear intentions for your personal development. Define areas of your life where you seek mastery and growth. Use the principles of Cause and Effect and Correspondence to align your goals with the universal currents of creation.

3. Celebrate Progress, Learn from Challenges

Celebrate small victories along the way. Recognise that progress is a series of steps, and each step contributes to the larger journey. Embrace challenges as opportunities for growth, applying the Alchemical Process to transmute difficulties into wisdom.

4. Connect with Community

Seek connection with a community of like-minded individuals. Share your journey, learn from others, and collectively embody the Principle of Gender by fostering collaborative partnerships on the path to self-mastery.

5. Embrace the Fluidity of Growth

Remember that personal development is a fluid and dynamic process. Embrace the Principle of Rhythm, understanding that growth involves cycles of expansion and contraction. Adapt and flow with the natural rhythms of your journey.

Living The Kybalion Code is an ongoing, transformative adventure —a journey of self-discovery, growth, and alignment with universal truths. As you apply the principles in real-life contexts, weave them into your daily routine, and draw inspiration from others' stories, you embark on a path that leads to a life harmonised with the profound wisdom of The Kybalion. May your journey be rich with insights, joy, and the alchemical magic of self-mastery.

How a Man Named Alexander Used the Kybalion to Transform His Life

Not so long ago in a bustling city, there lived a man named Alexander who felt trapped in the monotony of his daily life. He worked a mundane job, had strained relationships, and struggled with a deep sense of dissatisfaction. One day, while wandering through a dusty old bookstore, he stumbled upon a mysterious ancient book called the Kybalion.

Intrigued by its enigmatic cover, Alexander decided to delve into its pages. As he read, he discovered the seven Hermetic principles that promised to unveil the secrets of the universe. Determined to transform his life, Alexander decided to apply these principles in his daily existence.

1. The Principle of Mentalism

Alexander began by understanding the power of his thoughts. He practiced mindfulness and positive thinking, slowly eliminating negative beliefs that had held him back. As he focused on creating a more optimistic mental space, he noticed a gradual shift in his outlook on life.

2. The Principle of Correspondence

Recognising the interconnectedness of all things, Alexander started seeing patterns in his life. He understood that improving one aspect would have a ripple effect on others. For instance, as he invested time in building meaningful connections, he noticed improvements in his work and personal life.

3. The Principle of Vibration

Realising that everything vibrates at a certain frequency, Alexander began paying attention to his energy. He adopted a healthier lifestyle, incorporating exercise and a balanced diet. The increased vibrational frequency not only improved his physical well-being but also attracted positive opportunities into his life.

4. The Principle of Polarity

Accepting that life is filled with dualities, Alexander learned to find balance in every situation. When faced with challenges at work, he reframed them as opportunities for growth. By embracing both the positive and negative aspects of life, he found a newfound sense of equilibrium.

5. The Principle of Rhythm

Understanding the natural cycles of life, Alexander became more patient and resilient. During tough times, he reminded himself that challenges were temporary and that they would eventually give way to better days. This perspective helped him navigate through difficulties with grace.

6. The Principle of Cause and Effect

Taking responsibility for his actions, Alexander carefully considered the consequences of his choices. He focused on creating positive intentions, knowing that his actions would ultimately shape his destiny. This shift in mindset led to improved decision-making and a sense of empowerment.

7. The Principle of Gender

Recognising the masculine and feminine energies within himself, Alexander sought harmony between the two. He embraced his intuitive side and allowed himself to express vulnerability when needed. This newfound balance in his internal energies enhanced his creativity and strengthened his relationships.

As Alexander diligently applied these principles, his life

underwent a remarkable transformation. His career flourished, and he formed meaningful connections with others. The once dissatisfied man found fulfillment and joy in the realisation that he held the power to shape his own reality. The ancient wisdom of the Kybalion had truly become the guiding light on his journey to a better life.

EPILOGUE

Embracing the Eternal Dance

As we conclude our journey through "The Kybalion Code," we find ourselves standing at the threshold of a profound transformation. The wisdom of Hermetic principles has woven a tapestry of insights, guiding us through the intricacies of the mind, the rhythms of existence, and the alchemy of self-discovery. It is here, in the epilogue, that we reflect on the timeless truths we've uncovered and consider the path that lies ahead.

In the pursuit of self-mastery, we have witnessed the power of Mentalism shaping thoughts, the dance of Correspondence aligning actions with purpose, and the cosmic symphony of Vibration resonating through every facet of our being. The dance of Polarity has taught us the art of embracing opposites, while the rhythmic flow of life has reminded us that challenges are but stepping stones on the path to enlightenment.

Through the alchemical process, we have witnessed the transformation of base elements into gold—the transmutation of life's challenges into opportunities for growth. The interplay of masculine and feminine energies has unveiled the harmonious dance within, fostering a holistic expression of our true selves.

As we stand at the crossroads of past and future, we carry with us the philosopher's stone of self-awareness—a timeless tool for navigating the intricacies of existence. This stone is a reminder that our journey is not a linear path but an eternal dance with the universe.

The Kybalion Code is not a set of rigid rules but a living guide, adapting to the unique contours of our lives. In its pages, we have discovered real-life stories of triumph, practical tips for daily application, and the inspiration to embark on our own quests for self-discovery. It is a testament to the enduring relevance of ancient techniques in the modern world—a bridge connecting the wisdom of the ages with the aspirations of today.

As you close this book, may you carry the essence of The Kybalion Code with you—a compass guiding you through the ebb and flow of life, a key unlocking the doors to self-mastery, and a torch illuminating the path toward enlightenment. Your journey is an eternal dance, and with the wisdom of The Kybalion Code, may you move through it with grace, wisdom, and the alchemical magic of self-realisation. The adventure continues, and the universe awaits your harmonious steps.

AFTERWORD

Continuing the Alchemical Journey

As we reach the Afterword of "The Kybalion Code," it is not just the end of a book but the beginning of an ongoing alchemical journey. The wisdom contained within these pages is not static but a living, breathing force that continues to unfold in the tapestry of your life. This Afterword is an invitation to reflect on the insights gained, acknowledge the transformations experienced, and consider the perpetual evolution that awaits.

"The Kybalion Code" is not merely a collection of principles; it is a guide for self-discovery and a roadmap for navigating the complexities of existence. Each principle is a key that unlocks doors to profound understanding, inviting you to explore the depths of your own consciousness and the vast expanses of the universe.

Consider the stories shared—the real-life experiences of individuals who have applied The Kybalion Code to shape their destinies. These narratives are not isolated events but living proof that the principles within these pages have the power to transcend theory and manifest in tangible, transformative ways.

As you stand at the threshold of the afterword, ask yourself: How have these principles resonated with your life? What changes have you witnessed, and how have challenges become catalysts for growth? This moment is an opportunity for introspection, a chance to celebrate victories, learn from setbacks, and reaffirm your commitment to the ongoing journey of self-mastery.

"The Kybalion Code" is a tool, a companion, and a source of inspiration. Its principles are timeless, adapting to the shifting landscapes of your personal growth. Carry this wisdom with you, not as a set of rigid rules but as a versatile guide that moulds itself to the contours of your unique journey.

The alchemical journey doesn't end; it evolves. It is a perpetual dance with the cosmic energies that flow through the fabric of your being. The principles you've encountered are keys to unlock the doors of your potential. As you move forward, may you continue to embrace the dance of existence, aligning yourself with the universal truths that resonate with the core of your being.

In closing this chapter, remember that you are the alchemist of your life, shaping reality with the profound wisdom of The Kybalion Code. The journey is yours to navigate, the principles yours to apply, and the magic of self-discovery yours to unfold. May your path be illuminated with insights, enriched with growth, and harmonised with the eternal dance of the universe. The afterword marks not an end but a continuation—a perpetually evolving alchemical journey.

ABOUT THE AUTHOR

Wayne Devlin Bcaa

Wayne Devlin is a Manchester-based author devoted to researching and demystifying esoteric wisdom. Originally from Manchester, UK where he still resides with his beloved wife and family. Wayne boasts an extensive library of ancient texts, world religions, and publications from mysterious secret societies.

This life-long passion for studying occult knowledge and humankind's spiritual legacies ultimately inspired Wayne to decipher the cryptic 1908 text The Kybalion. After his wife, asked him what the Kybalion was about in layman's terms Wayne set to work. Recognising the little book's powerful but dense seven principles encoding the mechanics of reality as a hidden gem, he felt called to create an accessible guide unlocking its profound teachings for genuine truth-seekers today.

Thus born out of pure fascination and persistence, Wayne's premiere title "The Kybalion Guidebook" finally unveils the plain yet life-changing insights from this seminal Hermetic manual in easy-to-implement language. No longer must the keys to mastering oneself and one's world remain obscured by symbolism or secrecy.

When not diligently continuing his research or enthusiastically spreading illumination, Wayne enjoys quiet moments curled up with a blanket, cup of tea, and one of his vast collection of books near the fireplace beside his beloved wife who shares his passion for growth and living consciously. Stay tuned for Wayne's upcoming modern interpretations of other occult classics!

PRAISE FOR AUTHOR

In "The Kybalion Code," Wayne Devlin emerges as a masterful guide through the intricate corridors of ancient wisdom. His skillful interpretation and articulation of the Hermetic principles reveal not just a scholar, but a soul deeply attuned to the transformative power of these ageless teachings. Wayne's capacity to distill profound concepts into accessible and practical insights is a testament to his commitment to the reader's journey of self-discovery.

Devlin's narrative unfolds with a rare blend of eloquence and clarity, inviting readers to explore the mystical realms of Mentalism, Correspondence, Vibration, Polarity, Rhythm, Cause and Effect, Gender, and the Alchemical Process. Through his words, these principles cease to be esoteric concepts but become living, breathing companions on the path to self-mastery.

Wayne Devlin's dedication to those seeking personal growth is palpable on every page. His ability to convey complex ideas with simplicity and his knack for infusing the text with relatable anecdotes make "The Kybalion Code" an enriching and engaging experience for readers of all backgrounds.

In the hands of Wayne Devlin, The Kybalion becomes more than a philosophical text; it transforms into a practical guide, a companion for the modern seeker navigating the intricate dance of existence. This work stands as a testament to Devlin's passion, wisdom, and his sincere desire to share the profound teachings that have the potential *to reshape lives.*

As readers embark on this transformative journey, guided by Wayne Devlin's insight, they will discover not only the timeless wisdom of Hermetic principles but also a compassionate and knowledgeable mentor in the author himself. "The Kybalion Code" is a remarkable achievement, and Wayne Devlin's contribution to the understanding and application of these ancient teachings is truly commendable.

- SAM ANDERSON

PRAISE FOR AUTHOR

Dear Readers,

It is with great enthusiasm and admiration that I extend my heartfelt praise to the esteemed author Wayne Devlin for his groundbreaking work, "The Kybalion Code." This literary masterpiece not only showcases Devlin's exceptional writing prowess but also serves as a testament to his profound insights into the realms of self-discovery and personal empowerment.

Wayne Devlin's dedication to philanthropy is nothing short of remarkable, with a track record of extensive and successful charity work that speaks volumes about his commitment to making a positive impact on the lives of others. The tangible results of his efforts are evident in the countless lives touched and improved through his charitable initiatives.

Moreover, the multiple awards adorning Wayne Devlin's illustrious career are a clear reflection of the undeniable success and widespread recognition of his transformative system. These accolades serve as a resounding endorsement of the efficacy of "The Kybalion Code" in guiding individuals toward greater self-awareness, fulfillment, and success.

Devlin's ability to seamlessly integrate profound spiritual principles with practical, actionable steps sets "The Kybalion Code" apart as a beacon of inspiration in the literary landscape. His unique approach resonates with readers on a deep and meaningful level, guiding them on a journey of self-discovery that transcends the boundaries of traditional self help literature.

In a world that often seems chaotic and overwhelming, Wayne Devlin's wisdom, coupled with his philanthropic endeavors, stands as a shining beacon of hope and empowerment. "The Kybalion Code" is not merely a book; it is a transformative experience that has the power to uplift and enrich the lives of those fortunate enough to engage with its pages.

In conclusion, I extend my heartfelt congratulations to Wayne Devlin on the resounding success of "The Kybalion Code" and applaud his unwavering commitment to making a positive difference in the world. His remarkable journey, marked by charitable endeavors and accolades, is an inspiration to us all, reaffirming that true success is not only measured by personal achievements but also by the positive impact one leaves on the lives of others.

- JOSEPH GROUT

BOOKS BY THIS AUTHOR

The Kybalion Guidebook

Unlock the Secrets of the Universe

The Kybalian Guidebook demystifies the esoteric teachings from the cryptic 1908 text The Kybalion. This obscure book by the mysterious "Three Initiates" outlined principles explaining how reality and human consciousness operate - principles said to reveal the mechanisms by which miraculous feats and alchemy become possible.

These seven "Hermetic principles" have been hinted at for centuries behind closed doors of secret societies and mystical orders. Now in plain language, the Kybalian Guidebook makes this forbidden occult wisdom accessible to genuine truth seekers. With simplified explanations of the universal laws, the guidebook shows the reader how to apply these principles in everyday life to create positive personal transformation.

Written for both complete newcomers as well as longtime practitioners, The Kybalian Guidebook offers the definitive roadmap to navigating your way towards enlightened mastery over mind and reality. The explorer's compass that points the determined apprentice to unlocking their highest potential.

BOOKS BY THIS AUTHOR

The Kybalion Code

A Self Help Book for Modern Day Using Ancient Wisdom

Unlock the ancient secrets of self-discovery and personal transformation with "The Kybalion Code." Grounded in the timeless wisdom of Hermetic principles, this exceptional self-help book provides a profound guide for the modern individual seeking fulfillment and growth. Through the exploration of Mentalism, Correspondence, Vibration, Polarity, Rhythm, Cause and Effect, Gender, and the Alchemical Process, this book unveils a holistic approach to self-mastery.

Discover real-life stories of individuals who have applied The Kybalion Code to manifest positive change in their lives. From practical tips for daily application to a personalized road map for self-mastery, this book offers tangible insights into transforming challenges into opportunities for growth. Each principle becomes a powerful tool, allowing you to harmonize your thoughts, actions, and energies with universal truths.

"The Kybalion Code" transcends time, bridging ancient techniques with the needs of the modern person. Embrace the fluidity of growth, balance the dance of masculine and feminine energies, and embark on a transformative journey guided by the alchemical wisdom of the ages. This book is your key to unlocking the secrets of self-discovery, offering a fantastic and practical guide to living a harmonious and fulfilling life. Embark on a journey of personal alchemy and align yourself with the universal currents of creation. Your path to self-mastery begins here.

Printed in Great Britain
by Amazon

35698595R00046